The Ballad of Matthew's BEGATS

Published in Nashville, TN, by Thomas Nelson. Thomas Nelson is a trademark of Thomas Nelson, Inc.

Thomas Nelson, Inc., titles may be purchased in bulk for educational, business, fundraising, or sales
promotional use. For information, please email SpecialMarkets@ThomasNelson.com.

Editor's Note: The names in the song and book are as they appear in Matthew 1:1–16 of
THE MESSAGE: The Bible in Contemporary Language. Copyright © 2002 by Eugene H. Peterson.

Library of Congress Cataloging-in-Publication Data
Peterson, Andrew.
  An unlikely royal family tree : the ballad of Matthew's begats /
written and sung by Andrew Peterson ; illustrated by Cory Godbey.
      p. cm.
ISBN-13: 978-1-4003-0909-2
ISBN-10: 1-4003-0909-3
 1. Bible. N.T. Matthew 1:1-16—Paraphrases, English—Juvenile
literature. 2. Bible stories, English—N.T. Gospels. I. Title.
  BS2577.P48 2007
  226.2'09505—dc22
                                              2007005541

Printed in Singapore
07 08 09 10 11 TWP 5 4 3 2 1

An unlikely royal family tree

The Ballad of Matthew's BEGATS

Written and sung by ANDREW PETERSON
Illustrated by CORY GODBEY

THOMAS NELSON
Since 1798

NASHVILLE   DALLAS   MEXICO CITY   RIO DE JANEIRO   BEIJING

Did you know...Abraham and his wife, Sarah, were really old when their son Isaac was born. In fact, Abraham was 100 years old!

Did you know...Jacob's twin brother, Esau was covered by so much red hair, his parent's named him "Hairy" and his friends called him "Red"?

Isaac, he had Jacob.

Jacob, he had Judah and his kin

Jesse, he had David,

who we know as king.

Did you know...
David was the shepherd boy
who killed the giant Goliath?

David, he had
Solomon by
dead Uriah's
wife.

Did you know...Solomon built the Temple in Jerusalem? It took 30,000 men to cut trees, 80,000 stonecutters, 175,000 other workers, and seven years to complete.

Solomon, well, you all know him.

He had good old Rehoboam,

Did you know...Jehosophat had
28 sons and 60 daughters?

Followed by Abijah, who had Asa. Asa had Jehoshaphat, had Joram,

had Uzziah, who had, Jotham, then Ahaz, then Hezekiah,

Did you know...
Hezekiah, the thirteenth
king of Judah, was
a good king? He
removed places where
false gods were worshiped.

Did you know...Manasseh was the wickedest king of Judah? He rebuilt the idols his father had torn down.
followed by Manasseh, who had Amon, who was a man, who was father of a good boy

Did you know... Josiah was eight years old when he became king? He worked hard to bring the people back to God. He ruled Judah for 31 years.

named Josiah, who grandfathered

Did you know...Jehoiachin was a bad king, so God let the Babylonians conquer Jerusalem? They destroyed the whole city, even the beautiful Temple. Jehoiachin and 10,000 others were taken to Babylon as slaves.

Jehoiachin

who caused the Babylonian captivity

because he was a liar.

Then he had Shealtiel,
who begat Zerubbabel,
who had Abiud,
who had Eliakim.

Then he had Eleazar, who had Matthan, who had Jacob.

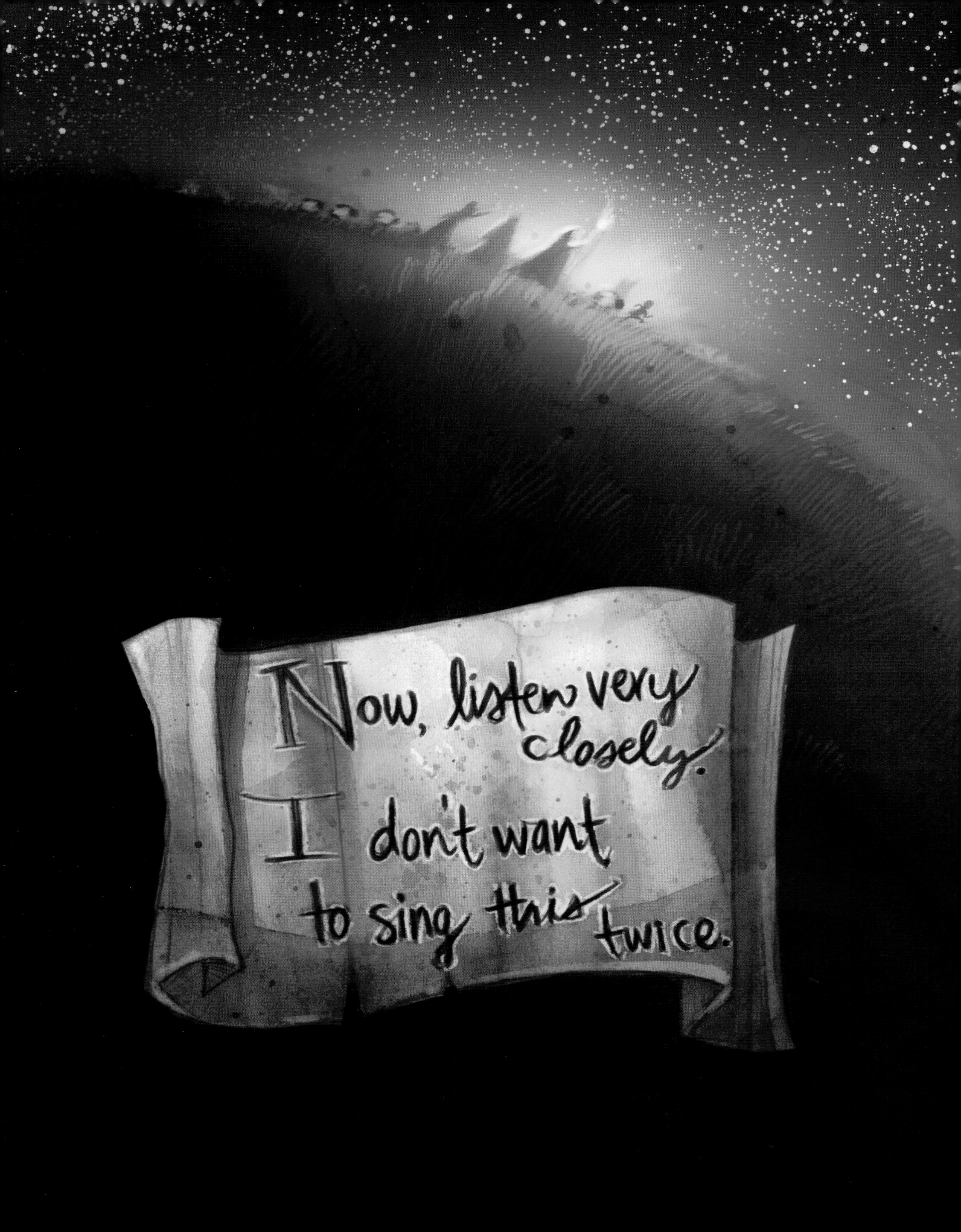
Now, listen very closely.
I don't want to sing this twice.

Jacob was
the father of
Joseph,
The husband
of Mary,
The mother
of Christ.

Did you know?

Rahab—Rahab lived in Jericho, which God was about to destroy. But when she helped some Israelite spies escape, they told her to hang a scarlet cord in her window and she would be saved.

David—Maybe the most famous person in the line of Christ, David killed the giant Goliath. He was called "a man after God's own heart." And even though he made a lot of bad decisions, he loved God.

Jehoshaphat—Jehoshaphat was the fourth king of Judah, and he liked to jump up and down a lot. Well, not really, but where else did we get the phrase "jumping Jehoshaphat"?

Manasseh—We don't know if Manasseh really swatted butterflies as shown in the picture on page 18, but it's likely since he was so bad.

Uzziah—Uzziah was king for a long time—fifty-two years. But one day he decided to burn incense on the golden altar in the Temple. This was a problem because God had strict laws that said only certain holy priests could do that. Uzziah didn't care. But God did and gave Uzziah leprosy because of his disobedience.

Josiah—Josiah, the grandson of Manasseh, became king at age eight. Everyone worshiped idols at that time, even Josiah. Then a priest found some old scrolls of the Bible. When Josiah heard God's Word, he repented, had all the idols destroyed, and worshiped only God.

Zerubbabel—Zerubbabel grew up in captivity, but later he led a bunch of Jews back to their homeland. When they got there and found it completely destroyed, Zerubbabel helped to rebuild the Temple.

The song "Matthew's Begats" was written one rainy summer afternoon when I was in that silly sort of mood that makes a songwriter want to put odd, often overlooked passages of Scripture to bluegrass music. Once the song was written, I set to memorizing it while I was washing dishes, perfecting my perpetual motion machine, pruning my bonsai tree, and eating apple crisp.

It took a surprisingly short time to memorize the song because, well, it's a song– and like most songs, this one rhymed, which was also easy to do since so many of the Hebrew names ended in "iah." In different Bible translations, some of the names have different spellings. For example, in my Bible, Matthew 1:11, says that King Josiah fathered Jeconiah. Well, there is also a little footnote that said, "That is, Jehoiachin," which was good news for me, because that name rhymed with "Babylonian" way better than "Jeconiah" did. Jehoiachin was a bad king, and his badness led to this really scholarly sounding tragedy called the Babylonian Captivity. Of all the evil things King Jehoiachin did, I'm sure lying was one of them, which gave me the perfect word to rhyme with his granddaddy Josiah. Well, almost perfect.

Why am I telling you these things? Because the song in this book isn't just a list of names. It's a list of people. Real people. People who were good and bad, and somewhere in between, and who were a part of God's great plan to redeem the world through another real person named Jesus. Just like you're a part of God's plan, no matter who your parents or your grandparents or your great-great-great-great-great-great-great-grandparents are.

I hope that while you're listening to this song and look-ing at Cory Godbey's wonderful pictures, you'll remember that all those stories you've been learning at church are true stories. And the good news is, because of Jesus you and I are a part of that story too.

ANDREW PETERSON
Nashville, Tennessee

Did you know that because of Jesus, you can be part of God's royal family, too.